Business Acumen

How-To Guides

CW00420708

How to Create a Business Case

If you only ever read one book on Business Cases, read this how-to guide by the Business Acumen Institute.

BY STEVEN HAINES

BUSINESS ACUMEN INSTITUTE

Contents

Introduction

Have you ever had a great idea that would help the company be more efficient or make more money? How do you go about organizing your idea, gaining the support of others, and presenting—with confidence—your idea to management? To get a solid sense of the traction it needs, or to work on a project that has been delegated to you, you'll need to become adept in the creation of a business case.

A business case is a standard method used to justify a company's investments. As a lawyer needs to make the case in a trial, so must businesspeople for business investments.

BUSINESS CASES CAN BE USED FOR:

✓ Facilities (buildings)

✓ Factories

✓ New or improved products

✓ Software and systems

✓ Market development

✓ Advertising programs

A business case is not a one-and-done exercise; it's a dynamic document that evolves as data are collected and analyzed so that an appropriate decision can be made. Incidentally, a business case is not a business plan. A business plan is a model for establishing an entire company that might be shared with a venture capital firm or financial institution. A business case has a singular focus: the investment to be considered.

Business cases are not usually done in a vacuum by one person. Often a small team of people, sometimes from different functions, will collaborate on the creation and presentation of the case.

Your credibility as a manager or leader may be tied to the creation of the case and for the intended outcomes. Therefore, it's vital to make sure that the business case isn't just an exercise to fill in the blanks of a template; it's to be carefully prepared and considered. Why? Because it's a reflection of your effort, and if the content is not grounded in facts or data, or if your assumptions are erroneous, your credibility may be harmed. In your capacity as a leader on a business case team, your role is like that of an investment manager with a fiduciary responsibility to the company. After all, leaders must protect the company from unwarranted risks.

The business case is designed to answer one or more questions that can be posed as follows:

Q: Should we move to another building because there are more people being hired?

Q: Do we need to expand production capacity to meet unexpected demand?

Q: Should we invest in a new product to become more competitive?

Q: Could we be more efficient if we automated one of our processes?

Q: Would we be able to improve our revenue and profit if we expanded into a new geographic area?

Q: Is a new training curriculum needed to cultivate business skills of emerging leaders?

To make the point clear, resources are scarce.

Different departments require investments to sustain and improve their own operations. Some of these are called out in their annual operating and capital budgets, or even in the agreed-upon initiatives set forth in the company's strategy. Yet, sometimes, just because the money is budgeted doesn't mean the chief financial officer (CFO) is willing to write the check.

Therefore, a good business case articulates the financial and business consequences for the investment over time with the rationale for quantifying benefits and justifying operating and capital expenditures.

Business Case Characteristics

A business case qualitatively and quantitatively rationalizes an investment, while considering elements that could include the needs of the business, proposed solutions, and economic outcomes.

1

A business case establishes a consistent model for rationalizing investments across the company.

A business case must be believable. The executives who oversee the company have limited resources and, often, limited patience. If you and your team present an incomplete business case, poorly crafted assumption sets, erroneous forecasts, or wild, unsupportable claims, you will probably not be asked back. Managers and leaders must always think about building their credibility horizontally and vertically within the organization—and the business case is a primary tool for doing so.

2

Business cases vary in size, scope, and level of effort, depending on the amount of investment and degree of risk involved.

A business case should be sufficient to put the point across. It doesn't have to be excessively long and verbose. Regardless of length, however, a business case usually undergoes several iterations before it has just the right blend of information.

3

A business case absorbs input from different people, including the most appropriate cross-functional team members.

Before you begin the business case, ground rules for document sharing and version control methods should be agreed upon by the team building the case. A business case team leader may assign a project owner to keep track of contributions, timing, and quality. It is the responsibility of that team leader to maintain control of the versions.

4

In assembling a business case, the assigned project team is responsible for the collection of data, associated analysis, and completion of the case.

The team should be cross-functional, with clearly defined roles and responsibilities, an underlying project plan for carrying out the work activities in preparing the case, and a target completion date. There is never enough time to be as precise as you and your team members might prefer. Team members must therefore be comfortable with the risks associated with making assumptions about scope, resource requirements, and financial forecasts. Many business cases are often unnecessarily extended over many months because of the quest for more and more accurate data. In those months, a lot can change. This could include an unexpected spike in demand, a new competitive product, or a shortfall in needed staffing. The team should attempt to strike a balance in terms of data collection, assumptions, risks, and recommendations.

> There is never enough time to be as precise as you and your team members might prefer. Team members must therefore be comfortable with the risks associated with making assumptions about scope, resource requirements, and financial forecasts.

Orchestration of the Case

The initiator and leader of a business case should have extremely keen insight into the firm's strategic goals, organizational dynamics, and political climate.

That individual must lead a team who can secure the cross-organizational buy-in required to support the investment. Just like an entrepreneur would pitch a venture capitalist, the business case leader must paint a portrait of achievable possibility.

When you understand this simple context, you can then begin to work the organizational backchannels. This includes having informal conversations with leaders in other functions as well as your own management chain.

Your great idea will not see the light of day unless you can convince the bosses that signing on to your program is worth risking their own reputation. Mere persistence and brute force are insufficient when it comes to securing funds for your project. Keep in mind that your idea is competing with a number of other initiatives whose champions feel that their project is most important.

Working with Senior Executives

It is crucial that you understand how your senior leadership team reviews the cases at hand and, ultimately, makes decisions.

This means that you have to figure out what their "hot buttons" are and how their decisions are made. You can do this by talking with others who have been through the process, including your boss.

You may also learn that some executives have their minds made up and are calculating what they need to do next without waiting for a complete review and final recommendation. This impatience can cause problems later on, especially if they or others have changed roles or left the company. Other executives may not want to go through the details of the case. Instead, they want to focus on the financials, or they ask, "What's the bottom line?" These are not responsible positions, yet it reinforces the need for a complete, accurate, and objective business case.

The best way to deal with this is to truly understand what executives are looking for and cover your key points early with detailed information as the story of the business case unfolds. This means purpose, scope, high-level financials, and the recommendation (even though the recommendation will be validated later in the case).

The Fundamentals of the Business Case

Regardless of company, industry, or idea, the business case should follow a fairly standard process. Sometimes a person who's assigned the case believes that the decision to invest is already made and that they're just putting the case together to bear this out.

Nothing could be further from the truth. Therefore, your mindset matters. You're responsible for the creation of a logical analysis and recommendation. A business case helps you and your team to say yes to projects that truly make sense and no to the ones that don't.

Every business case needs a team of people. Team members can include:

- The subject matter experts who work with you on the case.
- The people who will be responsible for carrying out what's recommended.
- The champions or the senior executive team who have a direct interest in the case recommendation.
- The beneficiaries or those who will gain from the outcome of an investment.

Every business case should be told as a story that you and your team are able to pitch.

All good stories have an engaging opening. For the business case, it's a problem or a challenge. The story starts, as all good ones do, with a problem. This is the business need you're trying to solve. Some examples: Are customers complaining about a product? Are executives unable to view product-level financial data because of an outdated accounting system? Have salespeople lost deals because it takes too long to sign off on a proposal? Alternatively, you may have attended a product line review and wondered why feature usage is dropping off on the flagship product. Regardless, when you have the proper background, you're set to construct the pillars of a good story.

Not all business cases are the same. How you choose to use this document and the template, the sections you include, and the time you spend depend on the purpose of the case. Many firms categorize business cases so they understand the staffing and level of effort required. These firms tend to use investment amount and level of risk as key parameters to divide into logical groupings. The table in Figure 1 below shows this type of categorization.

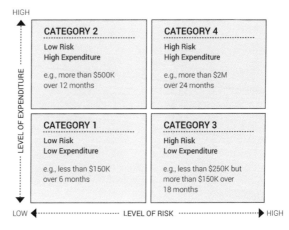

Figure 1 – Businesss Case Categories

Every business case involves a sequence of evaluative activities.

Most companies use business cases. Because the process may vary, it's a good idea to figure out how your company approaches the development and presentation of cases. You can work with managers, peers, or others as you network to grasp how things are done. Further, as mentioned earlier, the size, scope, and depth of business cases may vary. As indicated earlier, business cases are classified (see Figure 1). This might provide you with sufficient context for the amount of time you'll need to set aside to undertake the analysis and document your findings. As an example, you won't want to spend four months and write a fifty-page business case for a category 1 project.

Also, find out how frequently the leadership team reviews cases.

In some companies, cases are part of monthly business reviews. In others, the review process is less structured. You'll want to become familiar with what's going on in your company.

One last point on this topic: you cannot just show up at a business case review as a stranger. Effective leaders know who's who in the company, who's on the leadership team, and what they're concerned with. You can approach key stakeholders and have informal conversations about what you're working on. Ask opinions or for advice. Through your interactions, they'll get a sense that you're doing your homework and socializing the idea. In Japan the word nemawashi means informal socialization in garnering support for a project. (It also means that all decisions are made by group consensus, and it's difficult to get something accepted if the organizational higher-ups have not been properly briefed ahead of time).

It's a good idea wherever you work. You'll learn much about the culture of the company, leadership styles, and the things company executives care about. As you go through this process, you'll be more visible to others, and you'll learn who the key influencers are.

The Structure of the Business Case

What follows is an outline for the business case. It can be used as a template and adjusted as needed for each project that's encountered.

The template is divided into sections that most companies will use. Some sections may be relevant for a specific case, and some may not. The main idea is to use what's relevant for the kind of case you're to prepare.

The intent is to explain what's included in each section—not in extensive detail, but enough to provide sufficient perspective for you and your team.

Also, a portrait of a business case presentation will be provided to show you the "slides" you can use in a presentation of the case to your leadership.

THE STRUCTURE AT A GLANCE

- Cover page
- Signature page
- Executive summary
- Framing: situation review and funding request
- Contextual information
- Scenario planning
- Business impact
- Project proposal
- Product description
- Assumptions, forecasts, and financials
- Operations and implementation
- Risk analysis and contingency plans
- Recommendation
- Appendices

Cover Page

A formal document like a business case needs a cover page. A cover page identifies the business case and serves to communicate to the readers the name of the project, a product name (if needed), the names of the team members, a version number, a date, and anything else that may be helpful. If there's a category that your company might assign, be sure to note that on the cover page.

Signature Page

You may need a separate page to gather signatures of the main approvers of the case. It may be organized as shown here. Insert as many as needed.

_____	_____
Executive Sponsor	Date
Full name	
Title	

Executive Summary

The executive summary acts as an introduction that captures the essential elements of the business case. It also sets up the formal investment request by summarizing the situation, presenting assumptions, and providing a high-level financial profile. The executive summary is always the last page produced because the entire case needs to be completed before it can be properly summarized.

Framing: Situation Review and Funding Request

Every good story needs a strong context, and this section of the business case is where you set the stage for everything you want to say to management. In fact, this is the perfect section to tell a story about what you've observed, what's happened that caught your interest, or why the problem is so important to address. Even if the project was assigned to you, the main ideas or themes need to be fully understood by you and your team.

To properly frame the business case, the team needs to identify the problem or opportunity faced by the organization. If the problem were to be solved, what benefit would accrue to the company? Business cases can focus on resolving inefficiencies, gaining revenue, reducing costs, or other benefits that will ultimately be qualified and quantified in later parts of the case. Explain the business need in a clearly constructed statement that articulates the problem or opportunity. What happened? What situation was encountered? Why is it deemed important? Is there an impact on the ability of the company to achieve its strategic goals?

> Whether these are internal drivers for efficiency or the management of costs, or external drivers that affect customers or impact the company's competitive position, it's vital to provide sufficient context so that it's clear what's going on.

Finally, based on your understanding of the vision, goals, and strategies of the company, explain how this investment is aligned and why. To do this this, describe how the envisioned outcomes contribute to the goals of the company.

Once the background and history have been shared, close this section with a funding request. A formal funding request describes what is needed now and in subsequent years. An investment request might be worded like this: "We are requesting $500,000 this year to support the development and launch of the ABC product enhancement so we can garner 5 percent greater market share in the US market. After the product is released, we will need an additional $75,000 per year for three years for ongoing support."

Contextual Information

As discussed previously, there are different types of business cases. Use this section in a way that's applicable for your situation or the type of business case you're using. For example, there's no market assessment or product description for a case that is focused on a process improvement or an investment in a business automation system. What follows are two possible sections to include in your business case: a market assessment and an internal assessment.

Market Assessment

If your investment has an impact on the company's products, markets, customers, or competitive position, a market assessment is needed. For a market assessment to provide the best context, data are needed. The data must be backed by research and facts that lend credence to the reason for the case. Here's what's to be considered:

- Market segments on which the company is currently focused, or where it would like to focus. Typical broad segmentation is done around a business-to-business or business-to-consumer model. More detailed studies examine business-to-business-to-business or business-to-business-to-consumer. You'll probably want to work with your marketing department on this if you do not have the relevant information.

- Customers. When discussing customers, cases often talk about customer needs and preferences, or shifts in those preferences. Many corporate strategies focus on specific types of customers because they represent an attractive grouping within a market segment. For example, luxury goods companies focus on the psychological and social needs of customers with a high net worth.

- Industry environment, or sectors in which your company operates or where its customers operate. Industry categories might refer to categories such as financial services, transportation, industrial machinery, and software and technology. When discussing the industry environment, you'll want to describe how those market areas have evolved and whether they are hospitable to the object of the investment to be made, or if there are challenges in market entry.

- Competitive landscape. Your company competes with other companies to sell products and services. Competitive analysis includes an understanding of where your company is situated or positioned with respect to others in chosen segments or industry areas. Competitive analysis also covers such items as the products that compete for customers, the market share of each competitor, and the strengths and weaknesses of each that may reinforce the opportunity portrayed in the business case.

Data must be relevant and up to date to ensure that what's imparted is believable and relevant. Some quick checks with executives might add credence to your case. Additionally, this is where market timing may be discussed; for example, what are market conditions that make this an important, timely investment? When does the market need the product, or when should the company begin a promotional campaign?

Internal Assessment

If the intended investment is for something to be used or deployed inside the company, its context and purpose must be clearly articulated. Because there can be so many types of internal investments, your team should have strong representation from the functional areas where the need exists, as well as for those who will be involved in execution if the business case is approved. Be sure to note this on the cover page as well as in the situation review.

Ultimately, each case comes down to a situation that requires attention, where business results are suboptimal and new ways are needed to modernize, create efficiencies, reduce costs, or support broader strategic initiatives. If a company needed to introduce a new product but didn't have the current factory capacity, for example, the business case not only would focus on market assessment, but would also include some type of factory or facility expansion and information technology (IT) investments. All of these intricacies need to be called out in the business case.

Classifying Solutions and Alternatives

As the team constructs the business case and reviews the situation and contextual information, the problem should be restated and the solution articulated in this section. Solutions can fall under any number of classifications. To reflect on what was included earlier, these classifications might include:

- Facilities (buildings, building infrastructure, e.g., heating and ventilation systems)
- Factories to expand or update production
- New products to meet the needs of growing markets
- Software and systems (accounting, operations, payment processing, service delivery, etc.)
- Market development to gain market share
- Advertising programs to improve lead generation
- Automation of business processes to promote efficiency and cost savings
- Operations (order handling, service, management, supply chain efficiency, logistics and transportation, etc.)

In each situation, there's a possible solution. Within each solution area, various options may be available, and these need to be analyzed. Solutions to any situation might include the following:

1

PURCHASING THE SOLUTION FROM AN OUTSIDE COMPANY.
In some cases, it may be necessary to buy a solution. For example, if market demand is rising, and a production capacity increase is needed, new facilities, machinery, and staffing may be necessary. An alternative to purchasing new machinery could be to add a shift to a factory, if this is a possibility. As another example, if you're operating a software company, and quality assurance or product testing is being done by people, an automated system might be able to speed up testing and hasten product releases. Options for the purchase of solutions from outside the company must consider initial costs and ongoing, incremental costs over time versus the benefit to be received down the line.

2 BUILDING OR CREATING THE SOLUTION IN-HOUSE WITH CURRENT OR ADDED RESOURCES.

When a company that produces products (tangible or intangible) finds that there is a need in a market for a new product, executives have usually opted to develop the product with current resources or to add to the current workforce. If it's a software product, the company may choose to divert resources from other projects or hire additional resources. The business case would focus on incremental costs, incremental revenue, and profits. In another situation, a company may wish to add to its IT systems to process orders more efficiently or service customers more effectively. In this case, the company might compare the cost to create and sustain this solution by developing it in-house to that of using an external firm. Even in these situations, various pros and cons emerge that could include the management of costs over the long term or the risk of a supplier's business stability.

3 OUTSOURCING THE SOLUTION TO ANOTHER COMPANY AS A WORK FOR HIRE.

In this situation, the case would include engaging a firm to do whatever work is necessary. Outsourcing, however, is often easier said than done. Many firms, for instance, outsource software development to companies located in other countries. If a US-based technology firm, for example, outsources coding but keeps other functions in product management, quality assurance, operations, and so on, in-house, coordination can become tedious and time consuming. Quality may suffer due to rework from misinterpreted requirements and a lack of oversight. Over time problems may emerge that cost more money than the up-front savings may have revealed. It's important to understand all of the parameters involved in establishing, managing, and sustaining relationships with outsourced firms, especially when there's the usual churn and turnover in your own company.

4 DOING NOTHING.
A business case addresses the question What happens if we take this course of action? But you and your team need to consider the consequences of doing nothing. That will help you to articulate the business need when you present your case. For example: "If we keep using the same system, efficiency will continue to drop by 5 to 10 percent per year, adding costs to running the business. This new system will reverse that trend—in fact, we project a 10 percent reduction in system costs over the next three years."

Sometimes doing nothing is a viable option. That's often true of internal improvement projects. Suppose the operations group wants to modify its facilities upgrade program to provide increased connectivity for remote workers. The team developing the business case will include a do-nothing option to show stakeholders what costs they'll avoid by approving the project. They may have to answer questions along these lines: If we don't get in line with this growing trend, what workarounds will we need in order to keep our employees connected? Be sure your team always considers the "do nothing" or the status quo as part of your decision-making process.

Many executives don't like to be provided with one option, but they also don't want ten options. Your job is to present stakeholders with a few reasonable alternatives. This means you'll need to filter your list of options by asking and answering questions such as these:

Q:
- Which alternative costs the least?
- Which option takes the least amount of time to implement?
- Which option has the fewest risks?
- Which option delivers revenue faster?

Sometimes you'll have an alternative that will fulfill several of these conditions, but each opportunity you present should have at least one big thing going for it. Don't offer an obviously unacceptable solution in contrast to your preferred choice; it will appear contrived and will impact your credibility.

Once you've selected a few options, informally socialize these with some of the executive stakeholders. You'll want to assess their preferences before you invest time to evaluate all the costs and benefits. Also, when you present the business case, include a brief discussion of the options you rejected and why so they can see how your team arrived at its choices.

Scenario Planning

Regardless of the type of solution to be proposed, there are usually a few pathways to implement a solution. These are called scenarios. A scenario is simply a story line that depicts a future series of events. Some people like to use terms like "best case" and "worst case" to describe scenarios. These are not necessarily effective ways to look at scenario planning in a business case.

Scenarios in the business case should be properly structured. A well-constructed scenario makes it possible to examine in detail the pathway to fulfill the intent of the case. Even with details, it's often difficult to consider every possibility. Scenarios are built on a number of assumptions provided as statements or a story line.

Here's an example of how a scenario and some assumptions might be articulated:

"If we start investing in February, and if we complete the development by October, and we are able to start selling and processing orders in December, by the time we ship our first unit and send an invoice, we'll be paid for the first shipments in March."

There are a lot of connected assumptions and inherent risks here. For one, what if development takes longer? What if sales can't be trained on time to sell? What if the factory has a problem sourcing materials, causing a three-month delay in shipments? Will customers go elsewhere if the company can't ship on time?

The business case team must be able to come up with the right number of possible scenarios that can truly address the situation under study.

SCENARIOS CAN INCLUDE ITEMS SUCH AS:

1. Amount of money to be invested
2. Timing of initial investments (outflows)
3. Timing of inflows of money
4. Timing of benefits to the company
5. Size or amount of investments
6. Unit volumes for products
7. Pricing for products
8. People or business functions involved and when they're involved
9. Dependencies on or between people or business functions (including availability of resources)

In the section below entitled Assumptions, Forecasts, and Financials, scenarios will be more completely portrayed.

Business Impact

Your team's decision to create scenarios is one step in the process. However, how many scenarios are needed? To make a logical comparison to the current way of doing things (the base case), your team will benefit from at least two additional scenarios. Each scenario should be able to articulate the assumptions used in order to derive the final business impact. Further, to structure the content of the scenarios, you'll need to look at two dimensions, costs and benefits.

Costs include expenditures that are made to fund the investment and sustain the investment if approved.

Costs can include:

INITIAL COSTS
- Facilities (space, power, utilities, lighting, equipment, etc.)
- Production lines (actual production equipment to be acquired)
- Other capital equipment
- Software or systems to be acquired

OPERATIONAL COSTS
- Current salaries and benefits
- Increases in salaries and benefits
- Increases in travel
- Increases in software or system maintenance and support
- Increases in marketing, sales, operating, and other expenses
- Increases in maintenance, support, or new systems or equipment

Benefits can include:

IMPACT ON BUSINESS AND FINANCIAL PERFORMANCE
- Market share growth
- Accelerated cash flow
- Lower cost of ownership
- Price increases due to a better value proposition
- Improvement in gross margin
- Higher earnings per share
- Greater customer satisfaction

OPERATIONAL BENEFITS
- Increased productivity
- Shortened development time
- Improved employee engagement
- Accelerated through put on processes

The scenarios will ultimately be distilled to simple comparisons based on the assumptions that will form the foundation for the calculations provided in the section: Assumptions, Forecasts and Financials.

Project Proposal

There are two projects in a business case. The first is the actual project to construct, complete, and present the case. The second covers the actual work that is the purpose of the case. What's covered in this section is the project for carrying out the case.

Whether it's construction of a building, installation and turn-up of an operational system, or development and introduction of a product, a project plan is required. A project's success is defined by its ability to meet its objectives, within the specified time frame, on budget, and with the right level of quality. The project proposal must clearly identify the following, at a minimum:

- The resources needed from each functional department
- The timing when resources are needed
- The deliverables for which each function is responsible
- The dependencies between departments
- The timing for deliverables to and from specific departments
- The dependencies of specific deliverables on other deliverables

Project plans can be very detailed and should be so that roles and responsibilities are clear and costs can be effectively captured. However, when you're preparing the case, use a high-level summary of the project plan in the presentation so the executives can understand what's to be done. Using tools like Gantt charts and other visual tools can help to explain the project plan. Save the extensive details for an appendix if warranted.

Product Description

If this business case is for a new product, product enhancement, new design, or other product-related investment that will impact the revenue and market position of a product, you'll want to focus on content in this section.

A product description is needed to convey the characteristics of the product that are connected to the customer needs you've uncovered (in the section on market assessment). The description includes the following elements:

- Functionality (how a product works)
- Features (how functionality is carried out)
- User or customer experience (what customers do, feel, or see that engages them)
- Designs or styles
- Performance characteristics
- Technologies used or needed
- The value or benefit it delivers to the intended customer
- The competitive advantage it provides for, or positioning

Product managers often complete this section and usually rely on product requirements documents, customer narratives, or user stories to portray intended usage or desired experiences. The level of detail for the product description in the business case may vary. For a new product, it may be more comprehensive, while for an enhancement, it may be brief. It's recommended that if the description is too long, capture the major highlights in the body of the business case in this section, and put the details in an appendix. Regardless of the level of detail, of course, the product description should clearly reflect the customer value proposition and the intended competitive positioning.

> Regardless of the level of detail, of course, the product description should clearly reflect the customer value proposition and the intended competitive positioning.

Assumptions, Forecasts, and Financials

As described earlier, scenarios are stories about the future. A manageable number scenarios should be portrayed so that you can tell the story of how the investment will impact the future of the business. As you develop your scenarios, each story may be changed or altered slightly to reflect adjustments in forecast volumes, pricing, costs, and expenses— that is, your assumptions about the future. For each scenario, change only one or two variables at a time so that outcomes can be compared against a financial base case. The variables that are usually changed in the business case center on pricing, volumes, costs of goods, cash flow projections, selling cycles, discount rate, and expenses by department. They may also focus on the initial costs and cash outlays as identified earlier in the Business Impact section.

As indicated earlier, a business case should demonstrate an incremental benefit to the business. Whether its capacity, efficiency, or a new product, the CFO and chief executive officer are interested in incremental impacts on the business and a solid return on investment. Financial analysis is one of the most important parts of the case. As mentioned earlier, sometimes an executive leading the review will go straight to the numbers. The numbers do tell the story, even though the rest of the case needs to portray the complete story. The financial analysis should include:

- A profit and loss (P&L) projection based on the team's agreed upon assumptions, should the investment have a P&L impact.
- A cash flow projection, showing when money is being spent and when money is expected to arrive. Just because you think a sale is made in November doesn't mean that revenue can be recognized in that year or quarter. Your company's accounting or finance department can help you with "revenue recognition" rules.
- The capital expenditures needed to start, along with any ongoing or additional capital expenditures.
- The operating expenses needed to start and sustain the business incrementally.

- The discount rate used to discount cash flows (available from the accounting or finance department).
- The payback period, defined as the amount of time it takes to have enough money coming back into the business to cover the initial costs of the investment.
- The net present value (NPV), or the amount of the total value of the future cash inflows in today's dollars. This will be explained later.
- A break-even analysis, which is an important measure of investment effectiveness that shows where the cash inflows equal cash outflows. Break-even can be expressed in time or units of volume.

Developing Forecasts

Every business has to figure out how it is going to invest its limited resources, and business cases factor heavily into these decisions. Each forecast is a reflection of a scenario and set of assumptions. As mentioned previously and restated here, these items include:

- Amount of money to be invested
- Timing of initial investments (outflows)
- Timing of inflows of money
- Timing of benefits to the company (cost savings)
- Size or amount of investments
- Unit volumes for products
- Pricing for products

Unfortunately, many forecasts are inaccurate because the underlying assumptions are not connected to the true timing of monies moving in and out of the company or the timing and accuracy of benefits to be earned.

For additional context, consider forecasts that focus on market potential, sales volumes for products, and timing. Teams that examine market potential must consider a host of factors that include current market share, potential new sales that can be made from the salesforce, advertising programs that stimulate demand, and so on. Note the dependencies between sales and marketing.

With this in mind, this section should remind you that forecasts must be data-driven and properly timed so that they reflect the most realistic execution of any scenario.

Next, we'll turn our attention to an example situation that will help you to understand and visualize investments and timing.

Suppose your company wants to invest in a new product, along with an additional production line to produce the product. We won't define the product specifically but use this discussion to show how various forecasts could be created. We'll just call it "the new product."

The Story: The marketing team has noted a drop-off in usage of the recent product in North America. Customers have communicated that their businesses are evolving, and that new designs and functionality would help them to improve productivity, which would also translate into the recognition by their end users. Company executives discussed this with the product team to come up with the new product to replace the old product. After an analysis of the situation, the product team worked with development, marketing, manufacturing, sales, and service to agree on two approaches to the development, manufacturing, and deployment of the new product.

Scenario 1 includes development, test, and launch in year 1 with sales ramping up through year 2. Because sales will start one year into the future and knowing that competitors are already working on their version of the new product, pricing will have to be consistent with the old product.

Scenario 2 includes accelerated development, test, and launch in six months with sales ramping up in years 1 and 2. In this second scenario, your company will have first mover advantage and will be able to charge a premium price.

With this, we'll assemble two scenarios. **One is The New Product: Scenario 1**, and the other, **The New Product: Scenario 2**. Each is shown as you a spreadsheet that resembles the format of a P&L statement. However, it shows the timing of inflows and outflows of cash by quarter and year and the resultant earnings before interest, taxes, depreciation, and amortization (EBITDA)—terms you should become familiar with and that you can learn from your company's CFO or financial texts.

Each will show only stand-alone incremental investments with varied assumptions over a two-year period of time, portrayed on a quarter-by-quarter basis for simplicity. Also, the calculation does not show discounted cash flow (DCF) and NPV, as these are calculations that can be applied by your CFO.

First, we begin with assumptions. Here we'll list the assumption categories:

Investments and Outflows

- Investments to develop the product, including staff for engineering and testing
- Equipment to be used in the lab to develop and test the product
- Equipment to augment the production line
- Marketing programs to update the website and create leads
- Sales training
- Customer service training
- Internal systems upgrades to accommodate ordering and billing
- Cost of goods to produce the product

Benefits

- Revenue (price × quantity)
- EBITDA (Earnings Before Interest, Taxes, Depreciation, and Amortization)
- Return on investment (ROI)—based on cash flow

With the story and assumptions laid out, the two spreadsheets mentioned for each scenario, and two graphs that follow will show the net cash flow for each option. To reinforce the point about this analysis, this is purely about cash inflows and outflows and treats both capital and operating expenses as inflows and outflows.

Return on Investment

Return on investment offers a vital view of the financial value of your business case. It's a simple way to measure the value of your case and offers executives an opportunity to view your case in relation to others. ROI is easy to calculate. The basic formula is shown here:

ROI = net benefit/total cost

You can work with someone from your finance department to help with this because there may be a system where you enter your financial information so that the right calculations are made. Of course, positive ROI is good, and negative means the project isn't worth doing. In the examples shown for New Product Scenario 1 and 2, the ROI is calculated by examining net positive cash flow versus the total investment of capital expenditures and operating expenses.

Payback Period

Payback period, one of the easiest ways to compute ROI, is a method that accounts for time and shows you how long it will take to "pay back" the money invested. You can create a basic payback spreadsheet that lists the total costs and benefits and spreads them over time, either by month or year. You'll determine period totals by adding up the inflows and the outflows of cash. Then you'll figure out the cumulative cash flow by adding period totals.

As the examples below show you, and as visualized in the graph, cash flow starts out as negative. When benefits begin to accrue, they'll offset those costs. The payback point occurs when the cumulative cash flow changes from negative to positive—that's when the cumulative benefits exceed the cumulative costs.

SCENARIO 1	YR1–Q1	YR1–Q2	YR1–Q3	YR1–Q4	TOTAL YR1	YR2–Q1	YR2–Q2	YR2–Q3	YR2–Q4	TOTAL YR2	TOTAL YRS 1-2
INFLOWS											
Financial											
Revenue						300,000	750,000	1,750,000	2,500,000	5,300,000	5,300,000
Cost of Goods						63,000	150,000	332,500	525,000	954,000	954,000
Gross Margin						237,000	600,000	1,417,500	1,975,000	4,346,000	4,346,000
TOTAL FINANCIAL INFLOW	–	–	–	–	–	237,000	600,000	1,417,500	1,975,000	4,346,000	4,346,000
OUTFLOWS											
Incremental Expenses											
Product Development	175,000	200,000	200,000	150,000	725,000	100,000				100,000	825,000
Marketing				120,0000	120,000	120,000	200,000	100,000	75,000	495,000	615,000
Sales Training				75,000	75,000				–	–	75,000
Service Training									50,000	50,000	50,000
Systems Upgrades						50,000	50,000			100,000	100,000
Equipment Maintenance						75,000	75,000	75,000	75,000	300,000	300,000
TOTAL EXPENSES	175,000	200,000	200,000	345,000	920,000	345,000	325,000	175,000	200,000	1,045,000	1,965,000
POTENTIAL CONTRIBUTION (EBITDA)	(175,000)	(200,000)	(200,000)	(345,000)	(920,000)	(108,000)	275,000	1,242,500	1,775,000	3,301,000	2,381,000
Capital Investments (CapEx)											
Plant Modifications	100,000				100,000						100,000
Machinery		600,000	–	–	600,000						600,000
TOTAL CAPEX	100,000	600,000	–	–	700,000	–	–	–	–	–	700,000
NET CASH OUTFLOW	275,000	800,000	200,000	345,000	1,620,000	345,000	325,000	175,000	200,000	1,045,000	2,665,000
NET CASH INFLOW (OUTFLOW)	(275,000)	(800,000)	(200,000)	(345,000)	(1,620,000)	(108,000)	275,000	1,242,500	1,775,000	3,184,500	1,564,500
RETURN ON INVESTMENT BASED ON CASH FLOW											36.0%

Figure 2 – The New Product Scenario 1

Figure 3 –
The New Product
Scenario 2

SCENARIO 2	YR1–Q1	YR1–Q2	YR1–Q3	YR1–Q4	TOTAL YR1	YR2–Q1	YR2–Q2	YR2–Q3	YR2–Q4	TOTAL YR2	TOTAL YRS 1-2
INFLOWS											
Financial											
Revenue			500,000	1,200,000	1,700,000	1,500,000	1,200,000	2,500,000	2,800,000	9,000,000	10,700,000
Cost of Goods			95,000	228,000	323,000	270,000	396,000	400,000	448,000	1,514,000	1,837,000
Gross Margin			405,000	972,000	1,377,000	1,230,000	1,804,000	2,100,000	2,352,000	7,486,000	8,863,000
TOTAL FINANCIAL INFLOW	–	–	405,000	972,000	1,377,000	1,230,000	1,804,000	2,100,000	2,352,000	7,486,000	8,863,000
OUTFLOWS											
Incremental Expenses											
Product Development	350,000	350,000	50,000	50,000	800,000	30,000	–	–		30,000	830,000
Marketing		75,000	75,000	75,000	225,000	75,000	75,000	75,000	75,000	300,000	525,000
Sales Training		75,000			75,000					–	75,000
Service Training		50,000			50,000			–		–	50,000
Systems Upgrades		50,000	40,000		90,000					–	90,000
Equipment Maintenance				50,000	50,000	75,000	75,000	75,000	30,000	225,000	305,000
TOTAL EXPENSES	350,000	600,000	165,000	175,000	1,290,000	180,000	150,000	150,000	105,000	585,000	1,875,000
POTENTIAL CONTRIBUTION (EBITDA)	(350,000)	(600,000)	240,000	797,000	87,000	1,050,000	1,654,000	1,950,000	2,247,000	6,901,000	6,901,000
Capital Investments (CapEx)											
Plant Modifications	100,000				100,000						100,000
Machinery		600,000	–	–	600,000						600,000
TOTAL CAPEX	100,000	600,000	–	–	700,000	–	–	–	–	–	700,000
NET CASH OUTFLOW	275,000	800,000	200,000	345,000	1,620,000	345,000	325,000	175,000	200,000	1,045,000	2,665,000
NET CASH INFLOW (OUTFLOW)	(450,000)	(1,200,000)	240,000	797,000	(613,000)	1,050,000	1,654,000	1,950,000	2,247,000	6,901,000	6,288,000
RETURN ON INVESTMENT BASED ON CASH FLOW											70.9%

NET CASH FLOW FOR TWO SCENARIOS

— SCENARIO 1   ••• SCENARIO 2

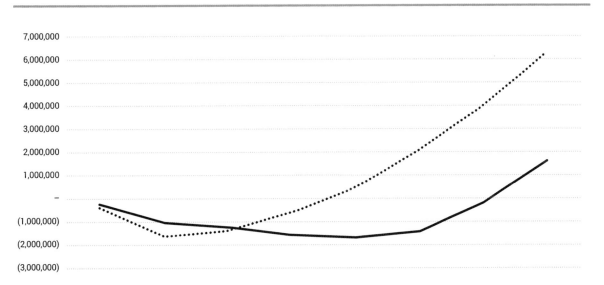

Figure 4 – Net Cash Flow for Two Scenarios

Scenario Analysis

A simple analysis of the two scenarios might cause you to believe that Scenario 2 is the best one. After all, the potential revenue and ROI for scenario 2 is much greater. Your company would get to market faster, and your market positioning would appear to be superior. However, there are some questions that need to be asked and answered:

- Are there capable resources available?
- Are any of the required resources committed to other projects?
- Can the factory equipment be ordered, delivered, and brought on-line on time?
- Will salespeople be adequately compensated for selling the new product?
- What happens if a competitor gets to market sooner?
- How is the overall economy, and will customers be willing to invest in the new product if the economic outlook is less appealing?
- Did anyone look into a build-versus-buy analysis to see if this solution can be outsourced?
- Will customers of the old product migrate to the new product?
- How does this investment compare to others that company executives are examining?

These questions and more should form the topic of debate within your business case team.

As the team collaborates and continues its research, the assumptions will surely change. That's why a business case isn't a one-and-done exercise; rather, it's a process that evolves as the team conducts its research. In a nutshell, it's about doing your homework.

Sensitivity Analysis

In forecasting and planning, the underlying assumptions may be subject to changes that can affect outcomes. You and your team may start to ask questions that start with "What if...?"

What if the cost of materials goes up in six months? What if we increase the price by 10 percent? Eventually, you will want to create additional assumption sets. Testing assumptions means that you change a variable (unit volume, a cost element, or a unit price) to assess the impact on future profitability. When you change a variable in the formula based on a revised assumption, you're trying to see how "sensitive" the impact is on profitability. This process is called sensitivity analysis.

When carrying out sensitivity analysis, you should change only one variable at a time. From this, you can see that variable's overall impact on gross margin or net cash flow. For example, if you believe that the most likely market situation will yield a unit volume of 1,000 units at $250 per unit for one year with revenue of $250,000, what happens if the volume is 20 percent less, and the price is the same? Then, the revenue would be $200,000. Would that be enough to sustain the business and deliver the targeted profitability, cash flow, and market share?

However, it's not advised to change variables to see numbers that look more favorable. You have to test the assumption that underlies the change in variable. Forecasting timing is difficult. When will the first order come in? What happens if we ship late and get paid late? How do all of these scenarios play out? This is why business cases are so dynamic; they require a lot of researching, hypothesizing, testing, and evaluating.

Evaluating the Financials Using Discounted Cash Flow

Throughout the year, many teams will propose business cases to the executive leaders. Because of the number of project requests and business cases to review, executives have to prioritize them based on the strategic intent of the company and the available funds for different investment categories. From another standpoint, the CFO, working with the executive leadership team, is supposed to take a portion of the company's profits, after providing for normal working capital requirements, and invest it. Regardless, any team that requests money is, in effect, borrowing it from the company and paying it back with interest (providing a rate of return).

This interest has another term in the corporate world: the discount rate. The discount rate is based on what is called the cost of capital. (If you're interested in this, you can read more about it in most finance textbooks.) Companies supply their checkbooks with money from a variety of sources, and each source has a different cost. The discount rate is also considered a function of the company's risk of loss— for example, if your product team doesn't pay the money back when expected. The discount rate may be increased for investments perceived as riskier. Suffice it to say that the CFO charges you a discount rate that accounts for the fact that money expected to arrive further into the future is discounted back to the present. Hence, we have the financial expression discounted cash flow. Here's a simple example of how this works:

Suppose your team needs $100,000 for a process improvement project that's expected to provide greater cash flow in the future. The finance department representative feels that the project has a low risk of failure and that the discount rate of 12 percent will be sufficient to cover the cost of capital and the relevant risk of the investment. Figure 5 shows how the cash flows are actually discounted. Let's see how this works.

	Current Year	Current Year +1	Current Year +2	Current Year +3	Total
Cash Invested	-$100,000				
Revenue		$45,000	$60,000	$75,000	$180,000
Discounted Cash Flow		$39,600	$46,464	$51,110	$137,174
Cumulative Discounted Cash Flow		$39,600	$86,064	$137,174	

Figure 5 – Discounted Cash Flow Calculations

- In the current year (CY), the team gets $100,000. In the first year, the net cash flow from product sales is $45,000. However, because it's one year into the future, the $45,000 needs to be "discounted" back to the present. In our example, it would be calculated as [$45,000 × 0.88 = $39,600], with 0.88 allowing for the discounting of the cash flow by 12 percent. In the second year (CY + 2), the product contributes $60,000 to the company.

- In the second year, the money is discounted twice (that's compounding the discount rate), which means it's discounted by 12 percent two times, calculated as [$60,000 × (0.88 × 0.88 = 0.7744) = $46,464].

- In the third year (CY + 3), the money is discounted three times, and the discounted cash flow is calculated as follows: [$75,000 × (0.88 × 0.88 × 0.88 = 0.6815) = $51,110]. Each future cash flow is discounted back to the present and then added up.

Adding up the future discounted cash flows is called the cumulative discounted cash flow (CDCF). Most financial analysts will take the CDCF and subtract the original investment to arrive at the net present value for the investment. Positive NPV means that the investment will generate a return to the business. The CFO and the executive team will likely compare different NPVs based on timing (cash flows received sooner are generally viewed more favorably), risk, and the absolute amount of the initial investment. This is an expression you will probably hear many times during your business career.

Operations and Implementation

In order to put the investment into action, several puzzle pieces must come together. Each investment has different parameters for deployment. This is why a good project plan is needed, and clearly defined roles and responsibilities can minimize risk.

For a product, it must be tested to be readied for launch. Product codes are needed, and the accounting and finance systems must be tuned to be able to process orders, send invoices, and collect money. Customer service must be able to handle complaints. Marketing must be able to develop lead generation programs, and salespeople must be compensated to sell. If there are legal and regulatory issues to contend with, sufficient lead time must be allotted.

For a process or system improvement, procurement may be involved in negotiating with vendors, and people in operations may need to create a physical environment for equipment and staff. Process documentation may need to be created, and training needs to be conducted. Then, there's usually a transition between how work was done previously and how it's going to be done in the future.

In some situations, people responsible for execution are faced with hard deadlines and budgetary constraints. Unexpected external challenges can pop up, including a shift in the economy, a technical glitch, or a legal challenge. The main point is to be sure that your team talks to others who may have done similar work to find out what could happen so that you can make the proper allowances.

Regardless of project type, the details must be examined so that resources can be properly deployed, and the envisioned benefit realized, with a minimum of risk.

Risk Analysis and Contingency Plans

The business case should represent the best possible proof that an investment will deliver the promised return to the business as established by key performance indicators (KPIs) and other metrics. One way of assessing risk is through both qualitative and quantitative (statistical) analyses of the major project elements or deliverables. A qualitative risk statement is, "What if development slips their schedule by two weeks?" Upon review of the project plan, the team then looks at all the cross-functional dependencies to see who else is affected and what happens with their deliverables. Again, this is the argument I make for good project management methods and tools that help track these dependencies. An answer to the question could be, "A day-for-day slip in the end date for the project," because all other functions are dependent on development's deliverable.

Quantitative risk assessments might also be made. Using a decision matrix, each milestone from each business function can be evaluated against specific probabilities of a problem occurring. What kinds of problems can actually occur? Here are some examples of issues that many business case teams have encountered and had to address:

- **Management Support Risk**—because not all managers will buy in based on their affinity to supporting certain kinds of projects and their influence and possible veto power.

- **Technology Risk**—because engineers and technologists often think the new method or tool will solve all problems, only to find that the technology was untested.

- **Deadline Risk**—because management imposes sometimes arbitrary deadlines, and the team cannot possibly do the real work necessary to validate the investment; if a "go" decision is reached, the project may immediately be in jeopardy.

- **Resource Risk**—because sometimes a function says, "Sure, we could do this," but when the project is approved, the resources aren't available.

- **Project Risk**—because there isn't an experienced project manager who can oversee the complexity of the program and keep all stakeholders to commitments.

- **Team Risk**—because sometimes the team doesn't work well together.

- **Complexity Risk**—because sometimes the project is so large and cumbersome that assigned resources cannot see all of the work that has to be done or don't have the skills to complete the work once it's identified.

These items represent just the tip of the iceberg. The lesson is this: the more you know about what can go wrong, the more careful you become about the business cases you commit to doing. Part of this lesson rests not in quantitative data but in the "gut feel" for the business, which is why the business case is such an important decision-making tool.

Recommendation

Every business case ultimately comes to a conclusion, and that conclusion is the recommendation, "Should we invest or not?" If so, why; if not, why not? This is one of the most important decisions that business case leaders and their teams make, and it is the reason you've been invited to present your case. Here's a hint: don't say yes when you mean no. So many of the people I have interviewed over the years have made this mistake. They did so much work on the analysis that even if the decision seemed to point to no, they recommended going ahead anyway. The idea behind the business case is to "green light" the right projects and to reject the wrong ones, regardless of how hard it was to arrive at that decision.

Appendices

The business case is built on vast amounts of data. It would not be reasonable to put every piece of data into the case because it would end up being too long. The appendix holds exhibits, charts, and anything relevant that serves as proof for representations, estimates, and assumptions presented in the case.

Kick-Start a Business Case

As you might surmise, the business case process can be complex and sometimes takes longer than you would prefer. It may also be a bit more difficult to get team members into a room for this kind of a project.

It doesn't mean they don't care; it just means that corporate realities sometimes force us to veer from the path a little to get the good jobs done. Here's an idea used by some companies to help get things moving.

First, do a little homework. Take the business case outline and begin to populate it on your own. You should always have a lot of research material around, so capitalize on that as well as other available content. The goal is to try to sketch out a great story line for the investment. Therefore, it's smart to do a lot of work on the framing section and situation review—to put the opportunity in perspective. Also, put some of the forecasting templates together, even if they're very rough.

You want to demonstrate to your colleagues that you can envision the future with the investment, if warranted. If you can show them that some of the work has already been done, it's easier to engage them. Your job as a leader is to do enough work so that you can get the main stakeholders into an initial discussion or meeting. This first step could also be used to rally the executives to dedicate resources to your team.

Next, meet with each needed person individually and discuss the project and some of the up-front work you're doing. This helps build consensus in advance. After you have a good draft, get a few close colleagues into the room from different functions and do some additional work or editing of the work you've already done. Leverage your collective experience and create a list of "things to look into." This sets the stage for people to begin conversations with others and to start to build consensus. Ultimately, you'll learn that there's an appetite for the investment that may not have seemed evident before. Alternatively, in a short period of time you'll reach the conclusion that the effort isn't worth pursuing.

Post-Business Case Analysis

You and your team worked exhaustively on the business case, and it was approved by the executives. Now that work has begun, and the benefits should be realized, are the results truly materializing?

You may be surprised, but most business cases are not audited or reviewed. There are many reasons for this, including employee turnover, other important work, or just that these audits are not part of the company culture. Yet if the case was approved, and people are doing their work, do you really need to do a look-back? Yes, you do, just as investors would want to see if their investment strategies are working. Whether it's a payback or cost reduction from a new system or the revenue and profit from a new product, teams need to audit the business case.

In general business terms, an audit is an evaluation or examination of a process, project, or system to determine how well all the internal elements performed together against the original plan. The word audit tends to remind people of a financial investigation, so some may be reluctant to use it. Nevertheless, people involved in the business case should have a formal, structured method to audit the business case results. The goal is a review of what happened in relation to the plan, including what worked, what didn't work, and the results that were achieved.

Here's the rationale behind this review: Every assumption that was set forth in the business case had a plan date or time when an expenditure was made or a benefit should be realized. The audit or review would determine whether or not what was planned actually occurred or whether there was a gap between what was planned and what actually took place. This is known as a gap or variance analysis. As part of the audit, your team could create a table that highlights key items in the business case.

These can include revenue, costs, and profits, for example. The table can include investment outlays or efficiencies to be gained. Whatever the items reviewed, the audit should be able to determine if corrective action is needed. In some situations, a revision to the business case may be called for to highlight what was learned and to recommend remediation.

Summary

Almost every investment opportunity in a company should have a formal business case. The business case documents the facts leading up to the investment request and presents the business, operational, and financial rationale behind the investment.

Business cases are not produced autonomously by a one person, but in harmony with a team of people from the appropriate business functions who can commit human and financial resources to carry out the actual activities that are the focal point of the investment. The business case is a true representation of—and ultimately, the archival documentation of—the company's portfolio of investments.

The business case evolves as various inputs are collected and synthesized into a meaningful story, which can be readily told by any team member who helped develop it. The contents, intent, and impact of the business case should not be a surprise to anyone, so it becomes a perfect vehicle for communicating across the business functions. Over time, you'll become more adept at doing business cases, as will others who will learn from you. The impact is undeniable. The company will more wisely invest scarce resources, and benefits that accrue to the firm can provide long-lasting, positive results.

Business Acumen Institute

Senior executives rely on their emerging leaders and managers to see the big picture of business and get things done. They want mindset and mojo, all in one! The Business Acumen Institute and its world-renowned training programs bring the complexity of the corporate world into clear focus so that people, across functions, can learn to:

- ✓ Think strategically
- ✓ Decide with data
- ✓ Act with Agility

- ✓ Build believable business cases
- ✓ Formulate actionable strategies
- ✓ Fulfill company's value proposition

To bring the world of business acumen into focus, a solid definition is needed. Business acumen is a portfolio of skills, behaviors, and capabilities needed to support an organization in the achievement of its financial and strategic goals. With this, and at the foundation of business acumen excellence is a model for how people think about business.

This multi-dimensional model, shown as The Business Acumen Canvas provides leaders and managers with the wherewithal to master each element, and to see the big picture of business.

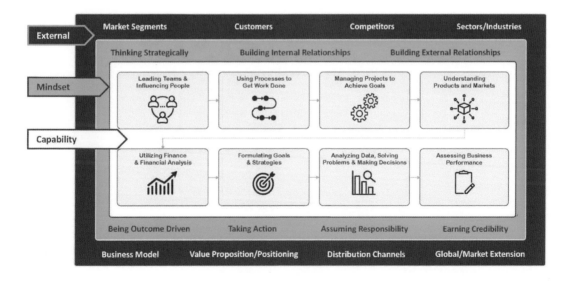

To download a digital copy of the Business Acumen Canvas and to learn more about the Business Acumen Institute, please visit: business-acumen.com

Printed in Great Britain
by Amazon

18710072R00027